Rivers into Islands

a book of poems by
John Knoepfle

Rivers into Islands

THE UNIVERSITY OF CHICAGO PRESS
CHICAGO & LONDON

Acknowledgment is made to the editors of the following publications, in which some of these poems appeared: *Colorado Quarterly, Calliope, The Critic, Commonweal, Deep Channel Packet, Delta Epsilon Sigma Bulletin, Epoch, Fleur de Lis, Genesis West, Inland, Midwest Quarterly, Midwest, Minnesota Review, Perspective, Poetry* (Chicago), *Poetry Northwest, Reflections, St. Louis Post Dispatch, Sponsa Regis, The Sixties, Queen's Work, Xavier University Studies, The Yale Review*

Library of Congress Catalog Card Number: 65-18338

THE UNIVERSITY OF CHICAGO PRESS, CHICAGO & LONDON
The University of Toronto Press, Toronto 5, Canada

For Peg

Contents

PART THREE

Part One

Part One

Good-bye, banjos

Good-bye, good-bye,
rebel rabble-rousing banjos
noisy as happily remembered minstrels,
undisciplined as southern revivalists.
Old age discriminates
the badger from the white-tailed deer.
Welcome to a peaceful country
delicate notes of bamboo flutes,
darknesses of strummed guitars.

Harpe's head

Harpe's dead.
He twangs hell's gut maybe.
He won't badger cabins
for new widows
or cheat sons of any more fathers.
We left the worthless part of him
fouled in mudflats
south of Redbanks,
but of Harpe's head,
we took that off gentle,
like a quail's is knuckled.
Goddam Harpe,
we spit there in the noon heat,
we'll wrap you up better than pharaoh.
We scooped stone ledges
below a creek bend
for blue cool clay
and thickened his flame of face with that.
It held him firm for Natchez
for some who knew him there,
down Ohio's shoaling
in a sloshed oak bucket.
Senators priced his took head
and cold-bedded women cursed it.
Oh, God, we booted that pumpkin
through Natchez-under-the-hill
until the blue clay cracked
and his withered head
leered at us.
Then we flung him
down a chuckhole full of blowflies
where hogs wallowed in the heat.

East St. Louis

Coal sells a bushel a week
at MacArthur Bridge.
Time weighs men by the peck
in the shacks there,
and the January dark
denies a summer delta.
Ice grinds the winter
river, a savage business.

Country sweat

When the flu came into town
a boy went quick. In three days
his father put him in earth.
The woman in the frame house
said evil could be circled.
She dragged her shaking daughters
off their beds and round the room
where death waited in the ring.

Some thought it was heat would drive
the sweat out and fat John Pike
who knew he was envied for
fifty acres on the bluffs
rinsed his children's feet of dirt
some neighbor charmed and made fires
for roasting off that June sweat,
but pine knots couldn't help him.

Lily Falmouth said it was
mirrors that gathered in germs
from miles around and she took
her looking glass in the dark
for fear of sunrise and drowned
her image in the river,
but death came swimming careful,
taking a shrewd look at her.

Some were wise and they had pots
they kept boiling on the bank
with river water kindred
dippered out to scald their heads
and some of these ran raving
that Jesus took up their lost souls

and others just lost their hair
and swore the water saved them.

The town druggist had his cure
for a man or canebrake boar.
Take headbust sucked with a reed
from an old oak charred barrel,
a pint of that, and then drink
his gin down with epsom salts
and store bluing. Some favored
that drink and others did not.

But no one dared swallow ice,
that was death in an instant.
So all the blistered summer
we watched each day how death came
with his black hearse and black team
while we spread out our dry hands,
and there wasn't any wind
plucking at the corn tassels.

Old woman's gift

We search
for the strange
laws of her anguish
and we come
to the great basilicas
where she
grew silent.

Diesel

This downgrade diesel
makes a nervous dark beyond
the pasture.
There were other whistles
I heard as a boy
where the trestle
framed the road at Red Bank Creek,
home-hungry sighs
that made my heart sad.
I could not tell the reason.
The click of the cars is the same:
gondolas sound an old theme,
steady in the late hour.

Those massive locomotives
pulling the heavy strings
lurched under bridges
into utter silence,
then with a whoosh
they clouded the shaken hills.
They were pile driving engines
and they died in my years.
The night is filled with whistles,
like an old freight in New Hampshire
sounding the travail of the race.

Street sounds

Charcoal cracks in the burner
where Kate and John and Carrie
dream at noon to a music box
that trails a firefly grace,
touching a light to their slender
needs. Wind in the locust
comes reeling on the edge of rain.
I hear the rash horns of fords
noising it up from a block away
where a bride comes soft from church
and billows in her silks, waiting.
Up on the next back porch
a woman slams her back door shut.

Pensioners in a park

Steeped in May roses
they sound themselves.
They are gnarled
and rooted as cedars.
Sitting on park benches
they are like thuribles
motionless in the hands of
yawning acolytes.
The rush of spring
tosses them about
in towers of their fragrant towns
like sunken bells.

Sparrows

In spring the men learn
how comforted the sparrows are
with six miles to feed on
from the river to the stone bluffs.

In July the men draw rakes
down seedless lawns,
combing bare dust in the yards
through curious designs.

In winter the ice storms lock
the grass the shrubs the trees
and the sparrows starve.
I have seen the men survive.

Late shift in the mill

The mill seethes
when the shift breaks.
Eyes of rats in smokeholes
burn ruby when the workers
throw crumbs to the walls.

The men pitch slag
that wounds the streaking
balls and claws.
They leave the cripples
dragging for the ravenous.

Arms bronzed, faces
stained in caves of fire,
they swing through miles of steel
the cold
carbuncular night.

Evening departure

She was afraid her fall might be
inevitable, her hands
tense with poppyseed for snow-starved
sparrows. She thought the pullman's
night would make her feel
close to the earth, so she
would rather go by train than fly.
I had no fears for her, which way,
shredding the black sunflower,
and when she said she would not care
if only I were holding her when death
was absolute, I laughed and scattered
the powdered seed. Why, thousands fly
day after day, I said, and they come home
for supper still, and wrecks of trains
are better news than known. Death
takes everyone, in good time too,
and she and I would have to die.

The porter saw her up his steps,
said wives part sad
and told me he'd take care of her.
He spoke like God confirmed his voice,
or the engineer.
I found her troubled smile.
Her hands were timid at the glass,
waving me good-bye.

Country night

Caw caw the crow cried.
The hound dogs woke to that
and the town dogs woke to the hounds.
Then the hounds were quiet
and the crow no longer cawed.

Alone on the bluffs
he comes in quiet.
The bluntheaded owl
has wind for wings,
his eyes two imperceptible moons.

Night of stars and flowers

Near the shadowy island
we made a wall for our war
with rambler rose and the lilac.

The gray dawn touched us,
and these were put away.

We saw a temple on the mountain,
all in rubble, washed in a blue wind.

And some of us stayed there forever
with the rambler rose, the lilac,
the blue keen wind.

Driftwood fire

I breathe
against the morning
some driftwood into fire.
The bank is dry
after late spring flood
and the Missouri
moves in princely darkness.

Now a man comes alone,
forming the mist he walks in.

I study him, intent
above my humming sticks
until I see the jugs he carries.

He will jug for channel cat this morning.
He will drift in a still world then,
the river bobbing with his jugs.

If I signaled him,
I know he'd come and sit awhile,
warm himself and weatherwise
the dawn,
but I do not make a sign.
Some disappointment
catches at his sleeve.
He's united states,
he has a hand in pocket want.

I turn my face to the fire.
A gust of wind troubles my light,
the flames swirl up,
and I am a digger of great tunnels
whose art cracks under
a universe of river.

John Henry

These moles came blind
up to freedom,
soot in a keen glaze,
cheap, where winter
slabbed the Mon'gahela
coal towns white.

They back alley'd
their hammering
that railroad through
the solid rock mountain.

And they laid their long
bones down in gin
and cursed a need for life.
In the rock below
the world was cut
to a common diamond.

The white mule

Coaltowns north of Pittsburgh have
old men with stump legs from the mines
or hands sheared who tell the children
there is a hunger in the deep pits,
a white mule one spent crew forgot
on a bad day for the mines. They tell
they have known it under the earth,
heard the hoofbeats ranging the pits,
then the lamps of the miners waver,
the men grow still, walled in their shadows.
They say the mule feeds on a lost man,
and they have known things it fed on.
There is a charm they have for hexing the mule
in the mines alone when courage wanes
and a man's heart listens to itself,
his echoes coming to join his own steps.
A man secures his life by turning.
If a man looks back the mule will vanish
when corridors pick up points of fire
from a bobbing, single lamp and the mule
comes softly down the tunnels of coal,
its eyes wide frozen on the lone lamp.
But these old men have never seen
the white mule, and as for the dead,
they were the men who would not look back.

At Marietta, Ohio

Where the Adena mounds were once,
men from Boston stockaded the bottoms,
and Putnam who mocked King George's army
led them there. They pioneered
with Indian worry, but grandsons read

the town paper to see what ships
were jamming for Asia. Welsh came after,
singing mostly through their noses,
but usually did not stay the town,
their craving still to the west for iron

farther along the valley. Germans
made a permanent coming, though,
and made the hilltops gutteral;
they would not trust a river fog
dissolving Muskingum's lower farms.

I knew a tough old man near there
remembered he pumped off bilges from
his father's flatboats. He said they sold
for boards to house the south—after
Vicksburg. His father sternwheeled back.

The old man clenched a hand to bring
him home. He said the fevered dead
were left at woodpile landings then
where no one knows how much of the nation's
hope lies buried in those graves now.

Keelboatman's horn

Why do you wake up the valley?
Put down your horn. We know
of others the river bruised.
They were sullen men
come back on the land.
The rainfog steeps your minor.
Let your conch shell
lose itself in the night.

Church of Rose of Lima, Cincinnati

It looks from the hill like something
Fra Angelico painted, the red
rectangular lines and the bricked bell
steepled out of time. This church
honors Saint Rose in a city
as spare of Peruvians as miracles.

It floods out whenever the river rises
and has a smell of common water
at the altars, and pilots of tows
on long hauls from Pennsylvania
needle the dark with searching lights
to catch the hour off her clock.

Saint Rose keeps a timid time.
I've heard her bell strike three
as if an afternoon surprised her.
The church itself may well surprise her.
In Lima she has golden altars; Germans
made them wood on the unliturgical river.

But churches anywhere seem rude for her.
This virgin kept a hidden time
and the world could give no wedding ring
to wed her with. Her lover came quick
and killed the Peruvian roses she grew fond of
and the small buds withered in the winter fog.

Once I thought the rococo Christ
had made her a violent dove and held
her trembling in his hand like a bell.
I am not so sure of this today.
She may be undiscoverable, like silt
slow rivers encourage into islands.

Part Two

The other night in Guatemala

They were wild dancers in their
feathers, yelling, "Gringo, gringo,
give us your dollars, gringo."
Well, I made a quick statement,
speaking a broken Spanish,
not knowing what Mayans said.
"I'm a student, not a gringo.
I borrowed that car," I said.
But they yelled, "Gringo, gringo,
we want your money, gringo."
I told them, "I'm a poor man,
and my wife and I without any change
were off to Costa Rica
for honeymoon when the rain
stuck us in this jungle road."
They said, "We do not like gringos."
"Fellow Indians," I said,
"Your natural respect
for family and home will sanctify
the ancient conjugal rites."
But they chanted "gringo" still
and one of them doubled on his knees
to spring a bright machete
howling through a circle
that jumped my head a little
when the blade sliced my neckbones through.
I caught the head in my hands
and cradled my palms to rock it
till both the eyelids fluttered shut

and the lips stopped quivering.
Then it spoke and said to them,
"Gringos, the whole trouble is
we didn't get enough plant food
for any deep roots."

October scrimmage

Below the office window
players stretch their cleats
over sweatsocks. They wear
promethean shoulderpads
this ancient afternoon, and I
can hear the murmur of their chatter
magnified down classroom brick
from where I crouch
within my cage of glass.
The team they play for
is famous in this town, and they
are all heroes. On the field
the scrimmage roars in dust
the wind whirls from the west
away, always from the west
away, and the sun there
wrinkles a shadow line of oak
against the school wall
in back of the boys who spit
on their hands and roll laces
to thread impossible eyes.

Prospector's grave

He is by the mountain,
his grave swept into a valley,
a lonely place, a man
lying face up to the west sky.

I think of a green grave
where there are no mountains.

Missouri hermit

The ramshackle man
was fond of his cave
and Indian pictures on a rock
west of the Mississippi.

He cured sassafras
and fingered the coins it sold for.
"Penny bread is good time drops."
He liked to say that.

He could spell out Greek
and told me, "Don't ever read
Thucydides, what happens
after Syracuse."

Beat poets

They spring awkward
from the belly,
snapping in the dark
for the civil nipples.
The mother screams
and doubles her knees
when they suck their pain.
The milk comes sour.

Riverfront, St. Louis

On the levee the Saarinen Arch
petitions luck for St. Louis
once and for all.
Cartons of trash
released from the Steamer Admiral
move in file on the Mississippi
with a kind of reverence.
Between cobblestones on the landing,
I discover a Roosevelt dime
blackened by many waters.

Hungarian Revolution

He is dead in the street.
His poverty
offers itself to the gutters,
a little poverty
still emptying from his wounds.

The machine gunner
can go home now,
secure on a mountain of silver.

We were watching,
great stone hands on our knees.

American fable

The mouse it is known
ferociously leaps
at the legs of a woman,
and scenting her hair,
the bat skirrs from his shadows.

These small creatures,
they are like children of negroes
who cringe along walls
when the big white cat
comes moaning on the stairs.

Night fire

Above the oil refinery
the torch howls in the wind,
flaring and contracting
among the millionaires.
It snaps there.
Smoke trails underneath it,
and I think it resembles
a severed head on a platter,
a John Baptist lurid in sparkles
of Bedouin handbells.
I drive down the road,
then it leaps up again,
grinning in the car mirror
like a colored porter in a plush hotel,
or a flame that roars in its solitude.

St. Louis midday

Sucking at summer
the black face
floats in the noon
heat. It moves
through hard dust and labor,
not conscious
of its own shadow.
It does not even know
the yellow lizards
crippled in its eyes.

He stacks bricks
in the hot day.
The headache ball
breaks down his home.

St. Louis midnight

These pale masks
sound on the wind,
crowding silences
of midtown avenues
until the hour
turns their wandering
where gothic homes
adjust them to
our sleep. Perhaps
they dream
in sober rentals,
white dwarfs
drifting in the universe.

Drifting

The long reach of the sea
rules him. He savored
the taste of good meat, wine,
taste of woman, nearness of
woman, multitudes
at his doorway, applauding.

That dreaming ends, the heart
broken to hunger, soul
risen from the locked legs
of the woman.
Slant gulls wheel the tides,
continents unreckoned.

Where the skull burns, nothing
tempers the wind, the sun
blazing on the sea.
Night hangs like a snapped string.
Hands slide from the tiller,
the boat leans in the drift.

Meeting in Chicago

A negro led me past
the Loop to Dearborn Station.
Said he never thought on
death, that debt, because
it came in any case. And he
removed from town to town
beyond identification.
Said I should forget
Chicago earth that breathes
my brother's life and where
the chi-rho marks his stone.

Holy Land

A man
drinks in his bar
at night,
looking
for someone.

It is
incomprehensible,
that city
of the swallows,
doves.

Edwardsville before sunrise

"Portals-of-prayer"
turns my clock radio on
and I am consoled
with the death of sparrows.
The bedroom windows are frozen
with obliterated stars.
A spider
embalmed in his ragged web
since the last September
is the king of that north.
My wife sleeps
a continent away.
Under the covers
my skin defines the strange
form of a man.

Old crazy fellow

He thought
how beautiful
these shadows were,
like feathers of doves
blown in the wind,
and he wanted to
bury them.

But the veins
of his sight
were scorched.

He wept because
there was nothing else
he could do,
sitting on a dunghill
of dead angels.

North on one-eleven

The swamp alongside the road
fed a world so dark
I could not see it
when I drove there each night
due north for home.
Sometimes a thin moon in the east
dropped shafts of light
on the steel rails that crossed the road.
I learned to watch for this light
gliding for the crossing
at precisely the speed of the car.

I would argue with myself,
the moonlight is without substance,
then feel it slam my stomach
and splinter in my nerves
when I hit the rails.

Later I remembered that light,
thinking of Augustine,
raw meat on the hooks of time
when Vandals were breaking the gates
at Hippo, and I told myself
it is the Vandals who are dead,
but the mouth of the old saint
gleams with foxfire.

Now tonight
the swamp fevers my road
and the moon is put out
and my headlights pierce the dark
with beams riven into banks of fog,
and I raise my arm
warding a blow.

Easter

I go with the others where
the priest the aging Sinai
mounts his tripled alleluias.

I kept my watch on a stone.
Now the stone rolls back.
I lie among chevrons ribbons eagles.

Wasn't I sent here to do something?
The priest stands in his place
and he shouts like a boy.

Heman Avenue holiday

When these georgian apartments are leveled,
bits of plaster clinging to the rooms we knew,
we will crawl naked from the stones of our cellars.
We will crawl up into the light, and among us
there will be pensioners and cooks and musicians,
and we will join together, as in a congregation.
We will not have any names and no identities.
We will have only our sadness for a little while,
the nipples yearning, secret whorls of the hair exposed,
the genitals designed with no further purpose,
the navels mysterious, meaningless, and we will go
and lie down in two long rows on the burnt grass
where the mall was with its cool green sycamores.
We will gather scraps of paper to rest ourselves on,
tissues, the halves of torn letters, school notes,
the waste of our generation on that long mall,
and we will pretend that if someone came with bread
we would not destroy each other for the broken crumbs.
No, we will die together in a greatness of our souls.

Part Three

October drought

The ensign at the flagstaff
ranges steady from the east.
The wind has blown dry
thirty full days now.
Grass underfoot is straw,
the sky sealed in a blue haze.

I tell you in these harsh mornings,
you sad bones of the dead
locked in the marrow of the earth,
I stand at noonday in my years
filled already with your riddles.

For a child who lived six hours

After the morning there was no noon
and now I leave your little white box
among the elms here. I give you back
with the harsh wind, howling
of the moonstruck dog, sleet,
rain, hail, the snow, the summer thunder,
wings that ruffle the air,
shapes of shadows in the deep waters.

Down Solomon

Ten days and south from Iwo,
a sea that calm you could have walked it
tiding the rare Solomons.
We knew the dead it held
were our own dead
and gave them silence under Savo.

My son reads this poem

My son reads this poem.
His six years
measure the length of each word
like a drop of pain.

I hold him against my chest.
I feel his small heart
straining to break my hands.

The washer of bodies: lines for Garcia-Lorca

After the soldiers with silver cockades
and silver pistols
taught him to die,
it was the moon came
to a place she knew
in Granada.
She found where his murder
was, that old woman,
her breathing heavy.
She found him in a pool
of silver.
Where she labored
in deep midnight,
birds sang the midnight
to the silver magnolia.

Sleep on an August night

I return to my bedroom,
walking five feet eleven,
and sleep there
in the bones and blood of myself.
Nothing happens in the night.
In the long darkness only the silence
worries at the lock
where the key is turning and turning.

Chipmunks

Chipmunks are ministers of war
on the rocks outside my cabin.
They dwell in the granite faults
among rubies and emeralds
and the bones of the dead.
They speak Chinese.

The sides of this mountain
are commanded with barbed wire.
The cabins are defended
with antlers of the former deer.

Mother of the hero

Where they found
his gravestone,
generals exhumed him.

She could not,
wondering,
take his bones in her lap,

or bundle
the white sticks
in her silk bandana,

or hide them
among spruce
in a secret valley.

Lines for my grandfather

I carried his ashes
on a Monday morning,
my grandfather
who could outshoot
Buffalo Bill.
He gave his pennies to the poor,
the ragged crowd
of my American dream
when he starved
among his children
in a New York flat.

The creating bear
ranges from a spoil of bees.
He slashes an oak
with his dripping paws.
His weak eyes burn
through an arc of swampfire.

Today if I remember the dead
I will visit the grave of my grandfather.
I will tell him let your ashes
rest in their heretical peace.

A man crosses his thigh with his forearm;
the plumb bob steadies on a point.

Hampton Road

Lean sabre jets
hatch in the fenders
of forgotten chevrolets
where teenagers
burning with the sun
crash through drive-in windows.
The radio
dredges an old channel
among obsolete songs.

Encounter on Delmar Boulevard

The stare of the blind man
shuffles up Delmar
with his tin cup and his bell.
His milky eye floats through me
and I know he cheats.
I see the Kennedy half dollars
grinding in his wallet,
great white-hot millstones.
But he cries, he cries
face the sun
with the blind man.
Eagles glitter in my sight.
They scream in piles of sticks
on the ledges of my eyes.

Old moon planter

We needed the moon.
Whipped our mules all day
while the sun whipped us,
and left those fields spilled
over sod with black
soil. And full mooned nights
we drove our wives there
yelling hi-ki-wee
ki-wee-ah and they
running like stark does
down that naked land.
And when they winded
we buckled their knees
and took them on top
those furrows milky
with their great moons full.
Then the green corn came
like mad I'll tell you.

Short note

The moon
has come up pregnant,
her belly
washed in the clouds.

Frogs
can swim on their backs now.

Only retired professors
will understand this.

Sisters

The hour is shattered.
The light swarms
on the green body
and the body drowns in a cup
with all the children
who cry in a sack
their death secures with a square knot.
Candles on the altars
nail the blood upright.
The sisters come to the wells.
They draw the waters
from the desolate places.

For a student

How old am I?
The rock is slabbed
beneath these acres.
Where the road curves at the entrance
that heavy rock falls
toward pyramids
no tractor will ever move.

And you, sweetheart?
Spring rain touches the young pine,
whippoorwills of light.

April return to Cincinnati

The evening too warm for April
takes me home.
The elm in the streetlight
hives for another
freshening linden and I consider
a darkness that is drifting
pale cherry blossoms on a small wind
over the hood of the chevrolet.
I thought that I had risen
heroic from such nostalgia,
that I had walked from my city
with absolute steps.
But I remember
only a man on a concrete bench
who is looking at the cinnamon river,
a brushstroke of the sunset
fading in the corners of his eyes.

June night on the river

Tonight the river is
calm enough. A string of cars
drums the long Eads Bridge
toward Union Station.
Pullman windows
charge the secret
spans of the bridge and tall
lights travel over the water.
They are hooded monks
gleaming among the piers.

Now I see whole mountains
honeycombed with monks,
and one of these, a boy
from Athos, fills the blue
Aegean with his own
image as he leans
beyond the prow of his skiff
and tries his luck
with a hooked line for his life,
his serious gesture.

The train goes its way,
the long lights
go out. I pour myself
a careful beer, tilting
a cold glass above
the Mississippi. It is
a lost river roiling
underneath the bridge. It came
from a deep cave on this
June night. And still it is

the one river Clemens
gave his own true Huck,
head buried in the black
knees of Jim, and the same
winds howl down streaks
of our summer storms.

Buffalo skulls

The skulls of the buffalo
remain. The circle of skulls
summons the herd, a medicine
that will not fail. They will come
from the north with the cold dawn.

And the night of their coming,
it has no end. Flowers
blossom in the eyes of the skulls,
then they wither
in those pale houses of the moon.

Men eat themselves
in the solid night of their dreams.
I do not want to stay
within this ritual circle,
or know my hunger in this poem.

Death after promise

The child
unfolding here is a butterfly.
Death after all promise
has come to me.

Now I walk in it,
its great gold wings
beating the air around me.

I cannot sell you my death.

It is a whole nation
forgotten by its fathers.